Germany's Spanish Volunteers 1941–45

John Scurr · Illustrated by Richard Hook

Series editor Martin Windrow

First published in Great Britain in 1980 by
Osprey Publishing, Elms Court, Chapel Way, Botley,
Oxford OX2 9LP, United Kingdom.
Email: info@ospreypublishing.com

© 1980 Osprey Publishing Ltd.
Reprinted 1983, 1984, 1985, 1987, 1989, 1991,
1994, 1995, 1996, 1998, 1999, 2002

ISBN 0 85045 359 3

Series Editor: MARTIN WINDROW
Filmset in Great Britain
Printed in China through World Print Ltd.

Among many works consulted in the preparation of
this book, the author found the following most useful:
Bueno, José Maria, *Uniformes Militares de la Guerra
Civil Española*, 1971, and *Uniformes del III Reich*,
1978
Davis, Brian L., *German Army Uniforms and Insignia
1933–1945*, 1973
Ezquerra, Miguel, *Berlin, a Vida o Muerte*, 1975
Infantes, General Emilio Esteban, *La División Azul*,
1956
Salvador, Tomás, *División 250*, 1954
Vadillo, Fernando, *Orillas del Voljov*, 1967, *Arrabales
de Leningrado*, 1971, and *Y Lucharon en Krasny Bor*,
1975
The author would like to thank the following for
their kind assistance: Museo del Ejército, Madrid;
Museo de Aeronautica y Astronautica, Madrid;
Servicio Histórico Militar, Madrid; and Mr Andrew
Mollo.

The author takes full responsibility for any errors in
his designs for the colour plates.

Artist's Note
Readers may care to note that the original paintings
from which the colour plates in this book were
prepared are available for private sale. All
reproduction copyright whatsoever is retained by the
publisher. All enquiries should be addressed to:
  Scorpio Gallery
  P.O. Box 475,
  Hailsham,
  E. Sussex BN27 2SL
The publishers regret that they can enter into no
correspondence upon this matter.

FOR A CATALOGUE OF ALL BOOKS PUBLISHED BY
OSPREY MILITARY AND AVIATION PLEASE CONTACT:

The Marketing Manager, Osprey Direct UK,
PO Box 140, Wellingborough, Northants,
NN8 4ZA, United Kingdom.
Email: info@ospreydirect.co.uk

The Marketing Manager, Osprey Direct USA,
c/o Motorbooks International, PO Box 1, Osceola,
WI 54020-0001, USA.
Email: info@ospreydirectusa.com

www.ospreypublishing.com

Introduction

In the early hours of 22 June 1941 Germany's armed forces were launched into war with the Soviet Union along a front of 1,600 kilometres which stretched from the Baltic to the Black Sea. Hitler's plan, Operation 'Barbarossa', envisaged a drive into Russia by three army groups—one striking towards Leningrad in the north, a second towards Moscow in the centre and a third towards Kiev in the south. He expected it to be a lightning campaign like those he had waged in Poland and France, and believed that in a few months the Red Army would be effectively destroyed and all Russian territory west of a line from Archangel to Astrakhan would be occupied.

Germany's principal allies in this struggle were Finland and Rumania, both of whom had been recent victims of Soviet aggression. They would later be joined by troops from Hungary, Bulgaria, Italy, Estonia, Latvia, Lithuania, Croatia, Slovakia, Albania, and even by Cossacks and hundreds of thousands of other volunteers from Russia itself. Volunteer units were also raised in the occupied countries of Holland, Belgium, Norway, Denmark and France. There was one other country that was not occupied by Germany, was ostensibly neutral and was not directly threatened by Russia, but that was none the less eager to send volunteers to a conflict which many people believed had begun in that country five years before—Spain.

During the spring of 1936 the ill-fated Second Spanish Republic had been disintegrating in increasing chaos and violence. In July the Nationalist forces of General Francisco Franco took up arms in what they believed to be a crusade against the anarchy and atheistic Marxism which were destroying the eternal values of traditional Catholic Spain. Amongst the mainly Monarchist and Conservative groups that rallied to Franco's

banner, the neo-Fascist party, Falange Española, had only a small representation at the outset; though the party grew in size as the war progressed, its actual power and its radical social reform programme were both carefully curtailed by General Franco (though he was later to implement his own extensive plans for social and economic progress). In addition to the professional soldiers of the Army of Africa and other regular units, Franco's army contained hundreds of thousands of volunteers from the civilian popu-

lation of the Nationalist provinces, approximately 200,000 of whom served in the militias of the Traditionalist Communion and the Falange. On the other side, half of the armed forces, supported by the Marxist and Anarchist militias, fought to save the Republic and occasionally fought each other. The vast majority of combatants on both sides were Spaniards, but the nature of foreign intervention makes it possible to regard the Spanish Civil War as a forerunner of the later Russo-German conflict. Soviet aid to the Republicans in war *matériel* and advisers, and in organizing the International Brigades, prolonged the war as long as it suited Stalin's foreign policy to do so. In recompense for this 'comradely' assistance, 510 tons of Spain's gold reserves were shipped to Russia, where they remain to this day. By April 1939, however, the small but effective German *Legion Condor* and substantial material aid from Germany and Italy had helped to secure Franco's victory.

Hitler's invasion of Poland five months later, and the subsequent declaration of war on Germany by Britain and France, brought Franco's confirmation of an earlier promise that Spain would remain neutral. In the months that followed the fall of France in June 1940, the Spanish leader skilfully resisted continuous German pressures and threats designed to force him to alter his position. At a personal meeting with Hitler at Hendaye, Franco rejected the German dictator's demands for a military alliance and permission for 20 German divisions to pass through Spain to attack the British bastion of Gibraltar. The events of 22 June 1941 introduced a change in Spanish policy, however.

The Blue Division

Conscious of a debt to Germany and a score to be settled with Russia, Franco and his Foreign Minister, Ramón Serrano Suñer, planned that a division of volunteers drawn principally from the Army and the Falange should participate in this new struggle. The prospect of striking back at Communism in its own lair enthused many Nationalist ex-combatants and young Spaniards from all backgrounds. They flocked to the recruiting stations, which had been established in the local headquarters of the Falange. In the Infantry Academy of Zaragoza the officer cadets volunteered *en masse*. By 2 July, when the recruiting stations were closed, the number of volunteers had been so far in excess of the 18,000 required that several divisions could have been formed. In a report to the Foreign Office in Berlin, the German Ambassador claimed that 40 times the required number had volunteered.

A general order of 28 June from Central Army Headquarters had stated that more than 50 per cent of officers and non-commissioned officers must be professional soldiers. In the event the percentage was considerably higher, and all officer grades above the rank of lieutenant were filled by regular officers. Four infantry regiments were formed under the command of Colonels Rodrigo, Esparza, Pimentel and Vierna; battalions were raised in Madrid, Zaragoza, Seville, Ceuta (Spanish Morocco), Valladolid, Corunna, Burgos, Valencia and Barcelona. An artillery regiment under Colonel Badillo, and units of reconnaissance, sappers, anti-tanks, signals and medical services were also formed. Of the men selected, nearly all were genuine volunteers. The colour of their Falangist shirts prompted the title by which the unit was to become universally known—the Blue Division.

To command the Division, Franco chose General Agustín Muñoz Grandes, formerly commanding general of the 22nd Division and Civil Governor of the district of Gibraltar. Muñoz Grandes was then 45 years old. He had commanded a corps during the Civil War and had been appointed for a brief period in 1939 as Secretary General of the Falange. Like Franco, however, he was not committed towards any political ideology.

On 14 July General Muñoz Grandes and his staff flew to Berlin. The remainder of the Division, after a farewell attended by military bands and cheering crowds, followed more slowly, crossing the international bridge from Irún in three trains per day, and singing exuberantly all

the way. Insults and stone-throwing by some French civilians only temporarily dampened the volunteers' spirits and, once in Germany, they received a warm welcome.

Blue Division officers and NCOs arranging provisions at Hendaye, July 1941. Note leather leggings, and shoulder-belts crossed at rear. Second from right wears three gold diagonal sleeve stripes of a sergeant. All wear the red beret; see Plate B. (Bundesarchiv, Koblenz)

From the 17th onwards the Spanish battalions began to arrive in the training camp at Grafenwöhr, near Bayreuth in Bavaria; and on the 25th the Spanish Volunteer Division was officially designated as the 250th Infantry Division of the Wehrmacht. In accordance with German divisional specifications, the number of infantry regiments was reduced from four to three. Colonel Rodrigo was appointed second-in-command on the staff and Colonels Pimentel, Vierna and Esparza now respectively commanded the 262nd, 263rd and 269th Infantry Regiments, each regiment having three battalions. The 250th Artillery Regiment contained three Light Groups, each of three batteries of 10.5cm guns, and a Heavy Group of 15cm guns. The Anti-

Tank Group was armed with 36 pieces of 3.7cm calibre. There was, in addition, the 250th Reserve Battalion, the Reconnaissance Group, Sappers Group and other supporting units of signals, transport, medical services, police and a veterinary company. Total strengths were 641 officers, 2,272 NCOs and 15,780 soldiers.

Intensive training began on 28 July. The German instructors were constantly irritated by their Spanish pupils' lack of smart appearance and reluctance to conform with German standards of discipline. On the 31st, the Division paraded to swear the mandatory oath of fidelity to Hitler, the wording, however, being modified

5

to specify obedience to the Führer only 'in the battle against Communism'.

After a comparatively short month of training the Blue Division departed for the front on 20 August. Trains bore them 1,200 kilometres to Suwalki in Poland, which they reached by the 26th. From Suwalki the Division set out on foot on 29 August to march through Poland and Lithuania as far as Vitebsk in Russia—a distance of nearly 1,000 kilometres. Whether the German Command's purpose was to delay the arrival of these noisy and undisciplined Spaniards at the front, or to toughen them up, was never made clear. Either way, the Spanish column endured a hard march, passing through Vilna, Molo-

deschno, Minsk and Orscha and leaving many hospitalized men and dead horses along the route. It was 40 days before the march was completed and the Division halted in Vitebsk.

By October the war was entering a crucial phase. Hitler's forces had won crushing victories over the Soviet armies on the central and southern fronts during July, August and September, when von Bock and von Rundstedt had carried out their vast encirclements of Bialystok-Minsk, Smolensk and Kiev, inflicting up to 3,000,000 casualties upon the enemy, including well over 1,000,000 prisoners, and capturing or destroying thousands of Soviet tanks and guns. The victory at Kiev, however, had been achieved at the expense of the original drive towards Moscow, which was halted when Hitler, rejecting all advice to the contrary, had despatched Guderian's armour southwards. Now, in October, when the Führer ordered the offensive against Moscow to be resumed, the weather had turned very cold; Army Group Centre, ill-

Artillerymen line up on a French platform, under a sign saying 'The German Army greets the Spanish Volunteers'. Prominent among their kit are the light brown ammunition pouches, aluminium plates, and rolled blankets. The khaki of their breeches varies in shade from one to another. (Bundesarchiv, Koblenz)

Artillerymen proudly show a red and black Falangist banner to two German infantrymen. The young gunner holding the Spanish national flag wears a Sacred Heart badge on his left breast. (Bundesarchiv, Koblenz)

equipped for winter warfare, would pay a terrible price for the imposed delay in the months that were to come.

It was now clear that the Spanish Division would not be going to Smolensk as was originally supposed, but instead would proceed to the northern front where Marshal von Leeb's forces had, from 8 September, begun to encircle Leningrad.

1941: The Blooding at Possad

After transport by train northwards to Shimsk, the first of the Spanish battalions moved into the front line on the night of 11/12 October to relieve the German 18th Division and part of the 126th. The Blue Division was now a member of the XXXVIIIth Corps of the 18th Army of Army Group North, and would be responsible for a front of 50 kilometres from Lubkovo on the west bank of the River Volkhov in the north, to Kurisko on the west shore of Lake Ilmen in the south. Muñoz Grandes established General Headquarters at Grigorovo to the north-west of the ancient city of Novgorod.

It was in the Division's northern subsector that enemy activity was at its strongest, and here the 2nd Battalion of the 269th Regiment fought the first action on the night of 12 October, within 24

7

A German Red Cross girl hands out cigarettes and confectionery to Spanish volunteers. The infantry branch badge can be seen on the collars; and the Falangist yoke-and-arrows can be made out in the original print on the left pocket of the much-decorated soldier on the right. (Author's collection)

hours of moving into the line. At Kapella Nova advanced Spanish positions surprised a Soviet battalion attempting to cross the river under cover of darkness. After nearly an hour of furious action the Russians withdrew, leaving 50 bodies lying in the snow on the river banks and 80 prisoners in the hands of the 2/269th.

The German Command planned to take the offensive on to the eastern side of the River Volkhov, employing the 18th and 126th Divisions and two regiments of the Blue Division. After two platoons had crossed the river at Udarnik and established a bridgehead on the east bank, the 2/269th crossed in force on the morning of 20 October, and by the 22nd had occupied the hamlets of Smeisko, Russa and Sitno. Soviet machine gun emplacements in the woods between Russa and Sitno provided tough resistance to the Spanish advance and there were several counter-attacks by large enemy forces of the 52nd Corps against Sitno. One attack, supported by artillery, penetrated to the centre of the village in the early hours of the 23rd. The 2nd Battalion's commander, Comandante (Major) Román, co-ordinated and led close-quarter fighting which eventually drove the Russians back, causing them heavy losses.

In the meantime, continuous Soviet artillery

barrages upon the river crossing points had failed to prevent the 269th from being reinforced. The 3/263rd occupied Tigoda on the 28th and Nitlikino on the 29th. Also on 28 October, the 250th Reserve Battalion had taken Dubrovka and then turned south to attack some strong stone buildings, instantly named 'the Barracks', in the suburb of Muravji. The Reserve Battalion was driven back by heavy automatic fire. Subsequent assaults on the 29th, supported by three Spanish batteries of 10.5cm, were unable to subdue the Russian defenders of 'the Barracks', whose machine guns decimated the Reserve Battalion until late in the afternoon, when the remnants were ordered to retire.

As November began the River Volkhov froze so solidly that heavy motor vehicles could safely drive across it. The Spanish units on the eastern side clung to their newly won positions under regular counter-attack by Russian infantry and continuous bombardment by artillery and from the air. On 8 November the Blue Division was instructed to occupy the small villages of Otenski, Possad and Posselok, which had been siezed by a regiment of the German 18th Division that had extended too far to the south. These three locations in fact lay 12 kilometres to the east of the present hard-pressed Spanish line on the other side of thickly-wooded terrain. Food and ammunition could only be supplied by means of a single road, frequently mined and under fire, which ran north-west from Otenski to Schevelevo on the Volkhov. The 1/269th was none the less given this task, and that same day distributed its companies, plus one artillery battery of 10.5cm, between Otenski, Possad and Posselok.

In the early hours of the 12th successive waves of Russian troops hurled themselves against the trenches and bunkers of Possad and Posselok. By 6am the village of Posselok was burning and the snow was littered with Spanish and Russian corpses. On receiving the order to fall back, the 40 survivors of the garrison withdrew northwards, fighting a rearguard action, to be greeted at Possad by a scene of exploding shells and burning houses similar to the inferno from which they had just escaped.

By the following day Possad was completely surrounded by the enemy. The remaining soldiers of the 1/269th desperately defended the outer circle of six kilometres of trenches, often driving back their assailants at bayonet-point. Soviet artillery continually pounded their positions. In the cellar of a house which had been converted into a hospital the wounded were heaped together until there was no room for any more. By the hospital door, and beside the entrance to the Command Post, were two ever-increasing piles of corpses that there was neither time nor energy to bury.

When 14 November dawned, 180 Spaniards still manned the defences while another 200 lay dead or wounded. Comandante Rebull arrived to replace the wounded Comandante Luque as battalion commander. His orders were to continue to resist. On the 15th Colonel Esparza ordered the sappers to construct two fortified positions, 'Intermediates A and B', between Otenski and Possad, in an attempt to maintain communications. After nightfall 200 wounded

were evacuated from Possad in a convoy of sleighs which had managed to pass down the road from Otenski, and the following night the survivors of six decimated companies were also relieved. Their place was taken by one company of the 2/262nd, another of the 1/263rd and a company of sappers. Comandante Rebull remained in command.

On 27 November two blockhouses were built to give increased security to the road between Otenski and Schevelevo. In the early hours of 4 December four Soviet infantry regiments, supported by artillery, mortars and aircraft, launched an offensive against all the Spanish positions

En route for Germany, a Wehrmacht soldier examines the Civil War medals of a volunteer, who also wears the Falange badge on the left pocket. The blue Falangist shirts are worn over the tunic collars. Note detail of ammunition pouch. (**Author's collection**)

east of the Volkhov. After being bombed from the air, the monastery at Otenski was surrounded by a Russian battalion. Comandante Román's two companies of sappers and anti-tank gunners, supported by two artillery batteries, fought for four hours before finally putting their attackers to flight. After nine hours the general situation in

Corporal of the Infantry Regiment 'Pimentel', later the 262nd Inf. Regt., with the 2nd Battalion's flag; Grafenwöhr, July 1941. See Plate B. The flag bears the legend 'Division Española de Voluntarios' above the device, and 'Regimiento Pimentel'/'II Batallon' below it. (Author's collection)

the Spanish bridgehead had been satisfactorily re-established except in Possad, which was still under attack by a massive Soviet build-up of forces. Possad had to be reinforced. General Muñoz Grandes had no alternative but to order the remnants of the 1/269th, reorganized in Schevelevo, to return at nightfall to the heaps of smouldering ruins and frozen corpses from which they had been relieved only two weeks before.

Possad remained under heavy bombardment throughout the 5th and 6th from aircraft, artillery, mortars and machine guns. The temperature dropped to 40° below zero centigrade. Oil froze on the bolts of the soldiers' weapons. What bread there was had to be divided with an axe, and the last potatoes had all been eaten. No-one had slept for three days and nights. Yet somehow they still managed to drive back the waves of Soviet assault troops which endlessly assailed the Spanish trenches. In response to calls to surrender the Spaniards yelled their Civil War battle-cry: *'Arriba España!'*

Muñoz Grandes was now authorized by the German Command to evacuate both Possad and Otenski. At 9pm on 7 December the last surviving defenders of Possad silently retired towards Otenski, a movement facilitated by the fact that the enemy had earlier fallen back in a similar state of exhaustion. From Otenski both garrisons marched off to the comparative safety of Schevelevo. During this epic month in the history of the Spanish volunteers the 269th Regiment alone lost 120 dead, 440 wounded and 20 missing.

In line with the decision of the German Command to reorganize units west of the River Volkhov with a view to intended operations there, by the morning of 10 December all Spanish units had crossed back over the frozen river to the line from which they had departed two months before. There was to be no respite, however, for the men manning the northern subsector.

Udarnik and Gorka both came under attack on Christmas Eve. General Muñoz Grandes had commanded the Division to hold its present positions 'as though nailed to the ground', and the Spaniards did just that. On the 26th Colonel Esparza ordered that a fortified position, called the 'Intermediate', should be established between

Udarnik and Lubkovo. The position was manned by a platoon under the command of Alférez (Ensign) Moscoso.

Early on 27 December sounds of heavy firing were heard coming from the Intermediate, which in fact was under attack by a Soviet force attempting to infiltrate to the rear of the sub-sector. At 6.30am Udarnik erupted in shell-fire, in the wake of which a Russian battalion managed to penetrate the village. Comandante Román's 2/269th drove the Russians out again and pursued them southwards. At the same time Comandante Rebull and three companies of the 1/269th were advancing northwards from Lub-kovo. At 10am the two units met at the Inter-mediate. They were horrified by what they found on the snow-covered promontory. Scattered around the trenches and weapon-pits were the bodies of Alférez Moscoso and his men, stripped of their uniforms, mutilated and literally nailed to the ground with their own bayonets and with picks driven through their chests.

The Spanish line was now almost re-estab-lished, but there was one more position to be recovered. A half-ruined church near Lubkovo called 'the Old Chapel' had been captured by a Soviet battalion. Comandante Rebull, supported by a German artillery group of 7.5cm guns, now furiously counter-attacked with two companies of the 1/269th. The Russian battalion offered little resistance and fled across the frozen surface of the Volkhov. From the west bank Rebull's men opened fire with an anti-tank gun and machine guns, supplemented by fire from the artillery and other nearby units. Within a quarter of an hour the icy surface was strewn with the bodies of the entire Soviet battalion. The atrocities of the Intermediate had been avenged.

1942: Lake Ilmen and the Volkhov Pocket

At the close of 1941 Germany's fortunes on the Eastern Front and begun to decline. On 5 Decem-ber Marshal Zhukov launched 100 mainly fresh

Spanish artillery officers with German instructors at Grafenwöhr, inspecting a line-up of 15cm guns. The red beret and Spanish shirt and tunic are still worn. (Author's collection)

Soviet divisions in a counter-attack against the 51 battered German divisions that had been halted at the gates of Moscow. Against the advice of his generals, Hitler ordered that his army must not retire a single step. As a result Army Group Centre was condemned to a frozen grave.

The Soviet High Command now also struck at the right wing of Army Group North. To the south of Lake Ilmen the German 290th Division was smashed by a massive Russian offensive. By 8 January 1942, 543 men of this division were still holding out in the village of Vsvad, which was surrounded by the Soviet 71st Ski Battalion. After telephone contact had been lost, the Ger-man Command requested that a unit from the Blue Division try to make contact with Vsvad and render aid. Consequently, on the 9th, General Muñoz Grandes ordered Captain Ordás of the 5th Anti-Tank Company to take command of the Ski Company at Spasspiskopez on the north-west shore of the lake.

At six the following morning the Ski Company set out through the darkness across the frozen lake. The company was 206 men strong. There were 70 horse-drawn sleighs, each with its own Russian driver, bearing ammunition and provisions for three days, five light machine guns and a pedal-powered radio. The thermometer registered 40° below zero inland, but on the open lake the freezing wind lowered the temperature as far as 56° below. The thick, snow-covered ice cap was formed unevenly, with many waves of solid ice which the sleighs could only cross unloaded, and with several deep crevasses which necessitated lengthy detours. As the march progressed throughout the day on a slow, zigzag course, more and more men lost all feeling in their feet, hands, noses or ears as frostbite struck them. The most severe cases had to be carried on the sleighs wrapped in blankets. Past midnight and into the early hours of 11 January the Spaniards were still struggling on through the

A volunteer photographed on arrival at Grafenwöhr; note rolled blanket, and the apparently improvised wound chevrons on his sleeve, their number suggesting long combat service—and appalling luck!—during the Civil War. (Author's collection)

fierce wind, up to their knees and sometimes their waists in dunes of snow. When the company finally reached the south bank of the lake it chanced to meet a German patrol from Ustrika. The exhausted Spaniards were at last able to take shelter in the cabins of Ustrika, after having been on the march for 24 hours.

In a morse transmission to General Muñoz Grandes at 10.10am Captain Ordás reported the arrival at Ustrika and that the Ski Company had suffered 102 cases of frostbite, 18 of them very grave. Muñoz Grandes answered that the Germans were still holding out at Vsvad and that the Ski Company 'must go forward until death'. Later arrangements were made with the Germans to evacuate the serious frostbite cases by ambulance to the hospital at Borissovo, where the treatment required by some would mean amputations.

During the next few days the company reconnoitred the coastal area to the east, where Captain Ordás established his command post at Pagost Ushin, and the terrain to the south-east. The temperature remained at 40° below zero and by the 14th the company had been further reduced by frostbite to 76 men. On the 17th Lieutenant Otero de Arce led 36 Spaniards and 40 Latvian soldiers of the 81st Division on a further reconnaissance to the south-east. Marching in a freezing wind through waist-deep snow, they passed through Maloye Utschno and Bolshoye Utschno, and first encountered enemy forces at Shiloy Tschernez. The Spaniards mounted an assault and drove the Soviet troops out of the village at bayonet-point. However, a foolhardy probe by two rifle squads to the next hamlet to the south, Pinikovo, resulted in the entire Spanish and Latvian force being put to flight and pursued northwards by six T-26 tanks and numerous Russian ski-troops. At Bolshoye Utschno Lieutenant Otero de Arce made a stand with a small group, holding back the tanks and skiers while the many wounded continued their

Symbolic photo showing men of the Blue Division crossing through a checkpoint on the German/Polish border at the beginning of their 40-day march up to the front. The bulk of the Division's transport was made up of these horse-drawn wagons. (Bundesarchiv, Koblenz)

flight north on sleighs until reaching the command post at Pagost Ushin. The lieutenant and a few exhausted survivors later made their escape under cover of darkness.

In the meantime, Captain Ordás had received an order that an advanced position must be established at Maloye Utschno. Consequently a group of 23 Spaniards and 19 Latvians, under the

Two Spanish junior officers on the Volkhov Front, dressed in German Army uniforms with the red and gold national shield on the right arm. The original print shows slight irregularities in the field caps: the left one has the silver piping extending all round the top of the 'turn-up' instead of just in the front 'scoop' as was normal; the one on the right has no eagle insignia on the crown; and neither seem to have the regulation silver crown-seam piping. The tunics are the 'economy' type with field-grey, instead of dark green collars. (Bundesarchiv, Koblenz)

command of two Alféreces, now departed southwards into the area from which Otero de Arce had just been forced to retreat. Early on 19 January the group's established position at Maloye Utschno was attacked by a mass of Soviet ski-troops, backed by tanks and artillery. Amidst shattered and burning cabins, Alférez López de Santiago, with the sparse remnants of his group, faced waves of assailants, primed on vodka, who were rushing into the explosions of their own grenades.

At daybreak Lieutenant Otero de Arce set out from Pagost Ushin with seven of his own men, a single 22-ton PzKpfw IV tank and two German platoons. Advancing through a howling snowstorm and under fire from Soviet tanks and machine guns, they were suddenly confronted With the limping figures of Alférez López de Santiago, four other Spaniards and one Latvian. Another surviving Latvian was later found crawling through the snow.

Captain Ordás now found that his Company had been reduced to only 20 men capable of fighting. The following day, the 20th, was the date fixed for Captain Pröhl and his besieged German garrison at Vsvad to break out silently after dark through the enemy encirclement. In the early hours of the 21st Lieutenant Otero de Arce started out eastwards accompanied by only a sergeant and five soldiers. At 5.30am, on hearing sounds ahead of them on the frozen surface of the lake, the group fired the agreed flare signal. After a moment the signal was returned and voices called from the darkness: 'Kamaraden! Kamaraden!' The Spaniards now rushed to greet the escaping garrison. Lieutenant Otero de Arce and Captain Pröhl shook hands and hugged each other. The mission of the Spanish Ski Company was at last completed.

With soldiers returned from the hospital at Borissovo, Captain Ordás found that he could now muster 34 men. To their dismay, the surviving Spaniards were required, three days later, to join German infantry of the 81st Division and several PzKpfw IV tanks in a drive to recapture the three villages to the south. In a temperature of 58° below zero, in which rifle bolts had ceased to function, the Spaniards fought with handgrenades in the vanguard of the column and occupied the final objective, Shiloy Tschernez, half an hour before the German infantry arrived.

On 25 January Captain Ordás made a radio report to General Muñoz Grandes of the strength of the Spanish Ski Company. Of the 206 men who had set out on the mission two weeks before, only 12 remained who had not been either killed or incapacitated by enemy action or frostbite. Captain Ordás was subsequently awarded the Individual Military Medal, and all others in the company the Collective Military Medal. The German Command also expressed its appreciation by awarding 32 Iron Crosses.

The Volkhov Pocket

From the end of 1941 the Soviets had begun to amass large forces on the east bank of the River Volkhov. In addition to the 52nd and 59th Corps who had been defending that front, the 2nd Assault Army was brought up with orders to effect a breakthrough which would achieve an eventual link-up with the 54th Army on the Leningrad Front. On 13 January 1942 the Russians attacked between Godorok and Dubvizy, penetrating as far as Finev Lug, Miassojbor and Ljubino Pole. The 2nd Assault Army then

In their first Russian winter the Blue Division had to improvise snow-camouflage garments from white sheets and—see hoods of patrol—shirts. These were effective visually, but of course provided no protection against the cold. (Bundesarchiv, Koblenz)

The field kitchens, like every other mobile support element of the Division, were dependent on sleighs during the winter months. It was with 70 single-horse sleighs of this type that the Ski Company set out on its hazardous mission across the frozen Lake Ilmen in January 1942. (Bundesarchiv, Koblenz)

poured through the narrow gap that had been created on the Volkhov, thus forming a pocket on the west bank. The German Command now notified General Muñoz Grandes that he must take some battalions of the Blue Division from their line and place them at the disposal of the German 18th Army for operations against the Russian forces in the Volkhov pocket. Consequently Comandante Román's 2/269th successfully relieved an encircled German garrison at Maloye Samoshie on 12 February.

By the end of March the rise in temperature was converting the previously frozen landscape into a sea of mud, which flooded the trenches and yielded up putrifying vegetation and thousands of decomposing corpses. The Soviets were by then convinced that they would have to evacuate the Volkhov pocket. Communications from the pocket to the east side of the river along destroyed and muddy roads had proved very precarious, resulting in scarcity of food and ammunition. The withdrawal was finally ordered on 1 May, at the same time as the German 58th Infantry Division and the 4th SS *Polizei* Division linked up to the north of the pocket.

As part of the German XXXVIIIth Corps' plan to attack the pocket from the south, Blue Division units in the northern subsector were provisionally aggregated to the 126th Division. At this time of year on the Volkhov the night only lasted two hours, from 11.30pm to 1.30am. In addition to temperatures of around 40° centi grade, the soldiers had to withstand the constant attacks of swarms of mosquitoes.

By the third week in June the Soviet forces on the perimeter of the pocket had been severely mauled by the German offensive, and the remainder were concentrated in a reduced pocket which was now to be attacked from the north, west and south. In the south, the 3rd Battalion of the 262nd and the 250th Reconnaissance Group became part of a grouping under the command of the German Colonel Burks, who had been given the mission of attacking Maloye Samoshie and linking up with other forces which would be advancing from the north through Kreschno. Burks's Group was composed of a German unit called the Valentine Battalion, positioned to the north-west of Dolgovo; the 3/262nd placed farther south on the eastern bank of the River Keresti; a Flemish battalion in position to the west of Ossiya; and the Reconnaissance Group, deployed to the north and west of Bolshoye Samoshie.

At dawn on 21 June the advance began. After progressing three and a half kilometres through thickly-wooded, marshy terrain, the 3/262nd was halted by intense machine gun fire from its left. That flank had been left uncovered by the slow advance of the Valentine Battalion. After bringing up anti-tank guns, the 3/262nd fought its way forward against fierce opposition. A former

Spanish Legion officer, Captain Milans del Bosch, led the way, refusing to be evacuated when he was hit by a burst of enemy fire. The battalion continued its advance until 4pm, when it halted at the small River Ossianka to the west of the objective, Maloye Samoshie; it was far in advance of both the Valentine and Flemish battalions, which had been unable to overcome Russian resistance. That day the 3/262nd had suffered 80 casualties. The other Spanish unit, the Reconnaissance Group, had been ordered to retire after a hard-fought assault against Soviet trenches in its path.

The following morning, in danger of being encircled, the 3/262nd also received orders to retire and fall back in an orderly manner. None the less, nine Spaniards were killed and 67 wounded by mines and constant harassment before the 3/262nd arrived back at its start line. Meanwhile the 1st and 2nd Squadrons of the 250th Reconnaissance Group had mounted an assault, with supporting fire from anti-tank guns and machine guns, against Soviet positions only a short distance from Maloye Samoshie. Raked with machine gun and artillery fire, and in the face of far superior enemy strength, the two squadrons eventually had to retire once more, having sustained nearly 50 per cent casualties.

On the morning of 23 June the intended attack on Maloye Samoshie began once more. This time Colonel Burks, from his command post at Dolgovo, ordered the Valentine and Flemish battalions to advance at any price and 'not to continue with arms folded while the Spanish advance

Convoys of horse-drawn sleighs were the Division's only effective mode of transport around the frozen-in villages on the Volkhov Front; they were the only means of taking supplies up to the line, and casualties to the rear. (Bundesarchiv, Koblenz)

Spanish soldiers keep watch from a trench leading to an underground bunker. (Bundesarchiv, Koblenz)

Reconnaissance Group made the final assault which secured Maloye Samoshie. The 3/262nd then spent three more days spread out through the malevolent woods and marshes, which were now full of rotting corpses, intercepting Russian stragglers still fleeing from the German push in the north. The Volkhov pocket was now liquidated. Colonel-General Lindemann, commander of the 18th Army, specially congratulated the Spanish units for the part they had played. In seven days the two units had captured 5,097 prisoners, 46 pieces of artillery and much other *matériel*, for which they had sustained 274 casualties. Altogether 32,000 prisoners had been taken in the pocket, all that had survived of the slaughtered 2nd Assault Army.

Far to the south there were other German victories. During three weeks in May 409,000 Russian prisoners had been taken at Kerch and Kharkov. On 3 July General von Manstein's 11th Army finally captured Sevastopol, completing the conquest of the Crimea. By 25 July German divisions had secured Rostov, the gateway to the Caucasus, and on 8 August General von Paulus's 6th Army encircled and smashed vastly superior Soviet forces at Kalach in the drive towards a city on the Volga called Stalingrad.

alone'. The vast woodlands trembled with explosions as German Stukas bombed ahead of the Reconnaissance Group, which pressed forward against Soviet resistance to a point just south of Maloye Samoshie. The 3/262nd, advancing from the south-west, had several encounters with the enemy and took hundreds of prisoners.

In front of Maloye Samoshie the Russians abandoned their outer defence line as the Reconnaissance Group, supported by four Tiger tanks, attacked.* The 3/262nd, the Valentine Battalion and the Flemish were all at that moment converging on the objective. The 11th Company of the 262nd was ordered to continue northwards to try to link up with the 266th Norwegian Battalion, which had been advancing from the northwest of the pocket. The three remaining companies of the 3/262nd reconnoitred the east bank of the River Keresti, flushing out entire Soviet units which had been wandering in the woods, most of whom were now ready to surrender.

At midday on 25 June the 3/262nd and the

1942-43: *Poselok and Krasny Bor*

It was also on 8 August 1942 that General Esteban Infantes arrived at Grigorovo to take up his appointment as second-in-command of the Division until Muñoz Grandes felt ready to hand over command. Until that March, Esteban Infantes had been Commander of the Military Region of Barcelona and had then been employed recruiting relief battalions, whose arrival

---

* If this identification is accurate, the PzKpfw VI Tigers were undoubtedly from *schwere Panzer Abteilung* 502, recently arrived at the Leningrad Front as the first operational Tiger unit. Editor.

Battery of 15cm guns of the Divisional artillery's Heavy Group. The 250th Regt. also had three Light Groups of 10.5cm weapons. (Bundesarchiv, Koblenz)

had since permitted parties of the longest-serving Blue Division veterans to return home to Spain.

Notification of an impending change of front raised hopes in the Blue Division of taking part in a great offensive against Leningrad which would finally link up with Finnish forces to the north of the city. On 23 August General Muñoz Grandes handed over the Division's sector to the German 20th Motorized Division. By rail and road the regiments and groups of the Spanish Division were transported from Novgorod to the area of Vyriza, which lay to the south of the Leningrad zone of operations. Here they became part of the XXIVth Corps, commanded by General Hansen. After a short period of training the Division moved north again to the Pushkin-Slutz zone to relieve the German 121st Division.

By 7 September the Division had occupied its new front-line positions in the environs of Leningrad. The city had been under siege since September 1941, when Hitler had decreed that the 3,000,000 inhabitants should be starved into submission. The Russians, however, despite appalling suffering from bombardment, hunger, cold and exhaustion, had continued to resist. There were 30 Soviet divisions trapped around Leningrad between the German and the Finnish armies. The Blue Division was initially deployed along a front of 29 kilometres from Pushkin in the west to Krasny Bor in the east. Muñoz Grandes established General Headquarters in the small palace of Pokroskaja.

Facing the Spanish line were three Soviet infantry divisions—the 109th, 56th and 73rd. The line was under frequent artillery, mortar and machine gun fire, which caused the Spaniards more than 20 casualties every day. In contrast to the Germans, the Spanish soldiers

19

quickly established friendly relations with the Russian population of the hamlets in the rear areas, particularly with the women, who came to the Spanish-occupied houses offering to do laundry, cooking and other domestic chores.

German motorized columns, Panzer regiments and batteries of heavy-calibre artillery were arriving continuously by night to reinforce the encirclement of Leningrad. General von Manstein, the conqueror of Sevastopol, visited Muñoz Grandes, and street maps of Leningrad were issued. Then the situation was suddenly changed by the setback at Stalingrad. On 19 November, as the German 6th Army was mounting another attack against the remaining Soviet positions in

General Muñoz Grandes being decorated with the Iron Cross 1st Class by General von Chappuis, commanding the German XXXVIII Korps; Grigorovo, 6 January 1942. Well known during the Spanish Civil War for his irregular uniforms, the Spanish commander is wearing an enlisted man's field cap without piping, and rank is indicated by a gold 'V' in the position normally occupied by *Waffenfarbe* piping. (Bundesarchiv, Koblenz)

that city, Russian armour smashed its way through the Rumanian 3rd Army on the Don, threatening the 6th Army from the rear. The following day, after the Soviets had effected a further breakthrough on Stalingrad's southern flank, Muñoz Grandes was informed that the offensive against Leningrad had been suspended. The newly arrived German reinforcements and artillery began to withdraw southwards.

At the end of November the Ishora and Slavianka rivers began to freeze and the Division once more found itself in a snow-covered landscape. Winter also brought seemingly endless nights, with the sun rising at 10am and setting at 2pm. On 12 December General Muñoz Grandes received a firm instruction from the Spanish Embassy in Berlin that he must hand over command of the Division to Esteban Infantes and return to Spain. The following morning Muñoz Grandes departed by air for Germany, where Hitler was to confer upon him the Oak Leaves to his Knight's Cross. General Emilio Esteban Infantes, after his long and patient wait, now took command of the Blue Division. The General was at that time 50 years old and, like his predecessor, had commanded a corps during the Spanish Civil War.

Commencing on 12 January 1943, the Soviets made determined efforts to break the encirclement of Leningrad by attacking to the east of the city and south of Lake Ladoga from both inside and outside the circle. The commander of the German 18th Army, Colonel-General Lindemann, ordered that each of his divisions must send a unit to help resist these attacks; and, on 16 January, the 2nd Battalion of the 269th was selected from the Blue Division.

The battalion, temporarily commanded at that time by Captain Patiño, arrived at Sablino on the 17th, and on the night of the 21st/22nd departed in trucks in the direction of Mga to the north-east. From Mga the battalion was directed northwards through the woods to a position south of Poselok, in order to relieve a battalion of the 162nd Regiment which had been badly mauled by a Soviet penetration. After marching under artillery fire in complete darkness and in a temperature that had dropped to 40° below zero, the 2/269th entered its front line positions at

3am on 22 January 1943.

At dawn the enemy bombarded the Spaniards with artillery and *Katyusha* rocket batteries, followed by bombing and strafing by Stormovik fighter-bombers. Unfortunately the so-called 'front line' had no trenches whatsoever, and the Spanish soldiers could only shelter as best they could behind trees, logs and mounds of snow. In the centre of the line, the 5th Company faced a charge by a mass of Soviet infantry. The company commander, Lieutenant Acosta, was killed by a bullet in the forehead, and the snow became strewn with dead and wounded Spaniards. As the enemy closed in, the remnants of the 5th Company fixed their bayonets and launched themselves at their foe. When the Russians fell back, the company was reduced to a quarter of its strength. None the less, the survivors managed to drive back two further assaults before being forced to retire from their position.

Muñoz Grandes chats with a Luftwaffe officer at Grigorovo; he wears the Knight's Cross which he was awarded in March 1942. (Bundesarchiv, Koblenz)

To the right of the 5th Company, the 7th had also been under heavy attack since dawn. The 7th's commander, Captain Massip, was wounded by shrapnel in the right temple during the artillery bombardment. He personally maintained a steady fire with a light machine gun at the enemy masses who bore down upon the company's positions and, when struck by a bullet in the left eye, fought on, refusing to be evacuated. After being hit yet again by a shot in the muscle of his left leg, Captain Massip stood up to throw his last hand-grenade and received a fatal bullet in the chest. He would be posthumously awarded the highest Spanish medal for gallantry—the Laureate Cross of St Ferdinand.

In the meantime, the 6th Company, like the

21

Blue Division officers at the Germany-vs.-Spain football match in the Olympic Stadium, Berlin, on 8 March 1942; the sports flag is in the red and black colours of the Falange. The score was 1:1. (Author's collection)

remnants of the 5th, had been forced to fall back as far as the battalion command post 500 metres to the rear; and at 3.30pm the 40 survivors from more than 200 men of the 7th Company were ordered to withdraw to the rear of the German 366th Regiment on the right. Captain Patiño calculated that, of his original 800 men, 600 were now casualties from enemy fire and frostbite. Despite this, he received orders that the Spanish battalion must counter-attack at midnight and recapture its lost positions.

Accordingly the remaining men of the 5th and 6th Companies drove the Soviets back in hand-to-hand fighting, and recaptured their previous positions by 10am on the 23rd. They were quickly surrounded, pounded by artillery and mortars, and stormed by wave after wave of Russian infantry. At midnight the survivors were relieved by German troops. The 2/269th—70 men, to be exact—was now pulled back to the second line; but on the morning of 25 January Captain Patiño was ordered once more to supply 60 men to occupy a threatened position in the front line.

Reluctantly he despatched Lieutenant Soriano, with almost his entire command, to a position where the Spaniards had to withstand several Russian attacks.

The following morning a Soviet artillery shell struck a cabin in the second line, wounding the six Spanish officers gathered inside, including Captain Patiño. Lieutenant Soriano was now the only officer in the battalion who was still on his feet. By nightfall he was defending his position with only 29 men. The enemy, however, had been heavily punished and a relative calm on the 27th continued into the 28th, when Lieutenant Soriano and his small band were at last relieved.

Two days later the Spanish battalion that had been brought up to Mga nine days before in 20 trucks made the return journey in only one. They arrived at the headquarters of the 269th in Slutz at 3.30pm—one officer, one sergeant-major, six sergeants and 20 soldiers. All were later decorated with the Iron Cross.

A tragedy on a far greater scale had meanwhile been unfolding in the Stalingrad pocket. By 3 February, after more than two months of siege in the grimmest of conditions, Field-Marshal von Paulus finally capitulated and 107,800 men of the German 6th Army and allied forces were marched off into Soviet captivity, leaving 80,500 dead behind them. About 6,000 of the prisoners would eventually be returned home.

Krasny Bor

During the first week in February reports were received of a Russian build-up of forces and armaments in the Kolpino zone. A Soviet drive south to try to gain complete control of the main highway and railway from Leningrad to Moscow seemed imminent, placing the section of the Spanish line to the east of the River Ishora in the greatest danger. It was just before midnight on the 9th that General Esteban Infantes received a telephoned report from General Kleffel of Lth Corps, to the effect that it was almost certain that an attack would commence the following morning, and that a regiment of the German 212th Division would be held in readiness to reinforce the threatened town of Krasny Bor if required.

Placed in position ready for the order to

advance against the right of the Blue Division's line were four Soviet divisions, the 43rd, 72nd, 45th and 63rd—44,000 men in total. Supporting these divisions were the 46th and 31st Armoured Regiments comprising 100 KV-1 and T-34 tanks; 187 artillery batteries of 12.4cm and 20.3cm guns; two battalions of 8cm mortars, two battalions of 7.6cm anti-tank guns, the 35th Motorized Brigade, and the 34th and 250th Ski Brigades. Awaiting this massive Soviet force, in poorly fortified positions, were 5,600 Spaniards of the 3/262nd, the 250th Reserve Battalion, the 2/262nd, the 1/262nd, the 250th Reconnaissance Group, and the Ski Company; the 1st Artillery Group, plus one battery of the 3rd with 10.5cm

guns and one battery of the 4th with 15cm; the Anti-Tank Group with 3.7cm guns and the Assault Sappers Group.

At 6.40am on 10 February the Spanish line erupted in flames and shrapnel as 800 Soviet guns commenced their bombardment. Artillery, mortars and *Katyusha*s pulverized the front lines and extended their range to the rear of the sector, destroying command posts, setting houses on fire

Three Spanish Army nurses of the 'Sanidad Militar' photographed with *Hitlermadchen* in Germany while *en route* for Russia, June 1942. They wear khaki blouses with nursing badges and decorations, with white collars and cuffs. Note unusual pocket design. (Bundesarchiv, Koblenz)

and throwing traffic into chaos. Despite being machine gunned on the road by four Soviet fighter aircraft, General Esteban Infantes managed to reach Raikelevo, where he discovered that the hospital was on fire but his advanced command post was still standing. From here he was able to direct the battle, as far as the ever-worsening communications permitted.

The artillery barrage continued unabated for three hours. The survivors in the practically destroyed trenches in front of Krasny Bor were then attacked by a total of 90 Soviet tanks, supported by massed units of infantry. Advancing in solid blocks, the tanks forced a breach between the 5th and 6th Companies of the 2/262nd and rumbled on towards Krasny Bor, much of which was now in flames.

By 8.50am the 3rd Company of the 1/262nd, defending the October Railway (Moscow to Leningrad), had already lost three-quarters of its original strength and was reduced to 40 men. Now, in the wrecked trench and bunkers along the railway embankment, littered with debris and corpses, Captain Ruiz de Huidrobo and his men faced a third assault by T-34 tanks and infantry of the 63rd Division. Hopelessly out-numbered, the captain called on his soldiers to fight to the last man. T-34s were now circling round to the rear and firing on the railway from the flank. As the enemy penetrated the right wing of the entrenchment, the Spanish survivors des-perately fought off their attackers with rifle-butts and bayonets. Captain Ruiz de Huidrobo led the resistance, firing his Parabellum pistol into the mass of Russian infantry who swamped the trench. Eight days previously he had torn up the pass which granted him leave to return to Spain to see his new-born son because he felt he could not leave his soldiers at a time when an enemy offensive was imminent. Now he fell with a bullet in his chest, and died after managing to murmur a short prayer. He would be posthumously awarded the Laureate Cross of St Ferdinand.

All along the line Spanish companies were being overrun by overwhelming numbers. On the left, the 250th Reserve Battalion had been almost totally annihilated. Of the 196 men of Captain Oroquieta's 3rd Company, only 60 remained unwounded. Trying to reach his decimated front-line companies the battalion commander, Captain Miranda, led a small group of headquarters personnel in a charge, singing the Falangist hymn 'Face to the Sun'. Submerged by an oncoming wave of Russian troops, they became yet another cluster of bodies lying in the snow.

At 10am some remnants of the 1/262nd managed to extricate themselves from the Soviet encirclement of their positions on the October Railway and fell back towards Krasny Bor. On the south-eastern margin of this town Captain Andújar counter-attacked with only 20 men of his scattered 2nd Squadron of the 250th Recon-naissance Group. Refusing calls to surrender, the section was overrun by forces of the Soviet 63rd Division, who shot or bayoneted any surviving wounded. Though hit by a burst of fire and then bayoneted three times, Captain Andújar was found alive an hour later by men of his squadron and carried to the hospital at Krasny Bor.

As midday approached, the situation was extremely critical. On the right, elements of the 1/262nd and the Ski Company were falling back, badly battered. In the centre, the 2/262nd had also been severely mauled, but a nucleus was still holding out. On the left, only two platoons of the Reserve Battalion were still resisting. To the rear of the front line the 3rd Sapper Company and the 8th Machine Gun Company, along with remnants of the 6th and 7th Companies of the 2/262nd, were regrouped and fighting bravely on the Moscow-to-Leningrad highway to the west of Krasny Bor. At Podolovo, on the west bank of the River Ishora, the 3rd Company of the 1/263rd and the 4th Machine Gun Company had pre-vented attacking Soviet infantry from crossing the river.

In Krasny Bor the 1st Artillery Group, the Assault Sappers Group and others faced a further attack by T-34 tanks and Russian infantry directed against the 262nd's command post and the hospital. The tanks fired their cannons and machine guns directly into the hospital, and shelled sleighs and ambulances loaded with wounded which were trying to escape south. Colonel Sagrado, commander of the 262nd, personally led a counter-attack to try to save the wounded. Men from a mixture of Spanish units desperately fought the tanks with hand-grenades

VOLUNTARIOS
FALANGISTAS
CONTRA "RUSIA"

1. Captain, Spanish infantry, June 1941
2. Falangist girl, June 1941
3. Falangist, June 1941
4. University militiaman, June 1941

A

1. Lieutenant, artillery, July 1941
2. Corporal, infantry, July 1941
3. Private, engineers, July 1941

B

1. Infantryman, winter 1941–42
2. Sergeant, Ski Coy., winter 1942–43
3. Cavalryman, Reconnaissance Group, winter 1942–43

C

1. Sergeant, engineers, summer 1942
2. Artilleryman, summer 1942
3. Lieutenant, Expeditionary Air Squadron, 1942

D

1. **General Muñoz Grandes, February 1942**
2. **Captain, infantry, 1942**
3. **Nurse, Sanidad Militar, 1942**

E

1. Standard-bearer, 269th Inf. Regt., 1942
2. Private, Inf. Bn. of the Ministry of the Army, December 1941
3. Private, Assault Platoon, winter 1942–43

F

1. Brigada, infantry, May 1942
2. Captain, Spanish Air Force, summer 1942
3. Lieutenant, infantry, May 1942

1. Chaplain, 1943
2. Grenadier, Waffen-SS 'Unit Ezquerra', April 1945
3. Company flag, 3rd Bn., 263rd Inf. Regt.

H

and bottles of petrol, and drove the Russians from the rubble of houses at bayonet-point. Just after 1pm the Soviets retreated and those ambulances that had managed to escape bore the wounded to a safer refuge at Sablino. At 2pm, far too late, squadrons of German fighter-bombers flew over the broken Spanish lines and began to bomb the Kolpino zone.

On the Moscow-to-Leningrad highway the 3rd Sapper Company had been surrounded for more than an hour by troops of the Soviet 43rd Division. Captain Aramburu decided to send Sapper Corporal Ponte to try to find a doctor for his many wounded. Corporal Ponte hurried down the road towards Krasny Bor, amongst a disorganized inferno of smashed sleighs and retreating men, under fire from enemy tanks and troops. He already had a bullet lodged in his body when he saw a T-34 suddenly separate from the rest of its formation and gain the road, firing its cannon into the Spanish soldiers, and seeming intent on driving towards the hospital. Despite being struck by a burst of enemy fire, Corporal Ponte took a magnetic mine from his pack and, ignoring the anxious protests of his comrades, staggered towards the tank and placed the mine between one of the wheels and the track. A blinding explosion destroyed both the T-34 and Antonio Ponte. Posthumously Corporal Ponte would be awarded the Laureate Cross of St Ferdinand.

As the afternoon continued, more centres of resistance were overrun. To the north of Krasny Bor 30 remaining men of the 5th Company of the 2/262nd ran out of ammunition and were overwhelmed. Four kilometres to the west the 3rd Company of the Reserve Battalion had withstood attack after attack, until the original 196 men were reduced to thirteen. Captain Oroquieta urged his men to resist to the last and was wounded for the second time that day. The encircling Russians then swept over the company's position and Captain Oroquieta and the other survivors were marched off into captivity.

Belatedly, at 4.30pm, a German regiment from the 212th Division moved to the northern edge of the Sablino Wood, extending to the west as far as the Moscow-to-Leningrad highway, while another German regiment advanced from Sab-

lino to link the first regiment to the east with Raikelevo to the west. These two regiments, reinforced by the Latvian and Flemish Legions, now formed a new division—the 112th.

General Esteban Infantes now ordered that all available Spanish forces must be deployed along the east bank of the River Ishora in order to prevent further enemy penetration and possible encirclement. The 3/262nd and companies of the 1/263rd and 2/269th had in fact been defending the River Ishora for some hours against powerful thrusts by tanks and infantry of the 72nd Division. Enemy attempts to cross the river at the paper factory in the loop of the Ishora, and south of Samsonovka, had both been repulsed.

By 5pm survivors from the 262nd, Anti-Tanks, Sappers, Reconnaissance and other units had abandoned Krasny Bor after more than 12 hours of fighting, and were retreating southwards through the Sablino woods. The only Spaniards now remaining in the town were principally men of the 1st Artillery Group, most of whom would make their escape at midnight. Also during the night, the remaining centre of resistance on the Moscow-to-Leningrad highway was relinquished by the approximately 150 survivors of the 3rd Sapper Company and the 7th and 8th Companies of the 2/262nd. After sustaining 23 hours of combat, they fought their way to the southeast until they reached the cover of the Sablino woods.

At dawn on 11 February 1943 Soviet artillery began shelling the paper factory and looped bend of the River Ishora. This subsector was defended mainly by the 3/262nd, and hundreds of men from the various smashed units of the original Spanish front line. A Russian infantry attack from the east bank was driven back just before 8am. Enemy pressure on the Ishora continued during the following days, and on the 15th attacks against Samsonovka and the paper factory were both repulsed with heavy Russian losses.

On the 17th Colonel Sagrado was able to render to General Esteban Infantes a full report of the action on 10 February which became known as the battle of Krasny Bor. The Division had suffered 75 per cent casualties in that sector (excluding the Ishora subsector)—3,645 total

Right centre, Comandante Julio Salvador Diaz-Benjumea, after landing from a successful mission. He commanded the 2nd Expeditionary Squadron from March to November 1942, adding two Russian aircraft to his score of 23 during the Spanish Civil War. Standard Luftwaffe uniform, with Spanish decorations. (Author's collection)

casualties out of 5,608 combatants. More than 300 Spaniards had been taken prisoner. The small territorial gain may well have cost the Soviets 11,000 casualties.

Three days later a long train left the station at Viarjlevo carrying a battalion of repatriates whose return to Spain had been delayed by the enemy offensive. The veterans left the front as they had left Spain—singing—and many were seen off at the station by tearful Russian girls from the rear-area villages. In the days that followed, enemy hostilities continued at a reduced level, which still occasioned the Spanish units in the Ishora subsector approximately 30 casualties daily. The last large-scale Russian attack came on 19 March. Artillery pounded the subsector before successive attacks by tanks and infantry were launched, principally against Putrolovo and the paper factory. All Soviet

assaults were eventually repulsed. After that day the defenders on the Ishora were subjected to fire from artillery and mortars, but to no further armoured or infantry attacks. Two months later the subsector was relieved by the German 254th Division.

Repatriation

Once more the spring brought mud, mosquitoes and decomposing corpses. The Blue Division returned to the quieter though still dangerous routine of trench warfare in fixed positions along its original front line, minus the Krasny Bor sector in the east and extending past Pushkin in the west. Opposite these 21 kilometres of line were emplaced the Soviet 72nd, 56th, 109th and 189th Divisions. Although the front was considered to have entered a period of relative calm, this still meant casualties for the Division numbering 300 to 400 per month from bombardment, sniping and trench raids.

From March until September 1943 there were regular monthly assaults upon the enemy lines by one company from each regimental sector, Colonel Rubio's 269th Regiment having most success in local attacks along the River Slavianka. These assaults were preceded by five minutes' artillery preparation, and it normally took no more than 40 minutes before the attacking infantry and sappers arrived back in their own lines, having blown up bunkers and fortifications and siezed armaments and prisoners. Soviet raids upon the Spanish lines were usually at night, and often at section strength, with the aim of capturing sentries. On occasion the Russians launched assaults by 200 to 300 men, which nearly always suffered heavy casualties.

At the end of July 1943 Soviet artillery bombardments increased in frequency and intensity upon the Moscow-to-Leningrad highway, and over the Antropschino-Mestelevo zone, where the Division had its hospital, workshops and stores. Partisans were also growing more active in the woods and hamlets of the zone, as they were in the rear of the entire Eastern Front, commensurate with the series of German defeats in August. The loss of Kharkov had followed upon the crushing defeat of von Manstein's offensive in the Kursk salient which, together with the disaster at Stalingrad earlier in the year, had finally sealed Hitler's fate.

With the threat of a Soviet offensive against the 18th Army the Division toiled in the heat of the summer months constructing a second and even a third defensive line of trenches and bunkers. This work was fairly well advanced when, on 5 October, Colonel-General Lindemann informed General Esteban Infantes that orders had been received to withdraw the Division from the line for rest and training. Earlier that day Soviet artillery had commenced a five-and-a-half-hour bombardment upon the positions of the 9th Company of the 3/269th to the east of Pushkin. The Russian infantry battalion which subsequently tried to storm the company's trenches was decimated by the 9th's machine guns and other automatic weapons. By midday the enemy had retreated, leaving more than 200 of their number dead. A second attack against the adjoining entrenchment of the 1/269th was also repulsed. This proved to be the Blue Division's last notable action.

Within 24 hours Esteban Infantes received instructions to transport the Division to the Volosovo-Nikolajeska zone and hand over the present sector of the line to the German 81st Division, supported by the 123rd. Esteban Infantes officially handed over command of the sector to General Schpper on the morning of the 12th, finally abandoning the line which had been defended at such cost, and where more than 2,000 Spaniards lay buried. The general's last visit was to the graves of his soldiers in the central cemetery of Mestelevo, after which he departed for his new headquarters at Nikolajeska.

Here, on the 14th, Colonel-General Lindemann decorated Esteban Infantes with the Knight's Cross, and confidentially informed him that the Blue Division would shortly be returned to Spain, to be replaced by a Spanish Volunteer Legion. Esteban Infantes correctly assumed that this impending withdrawal was due to the decided setback in Germany's fortunes, combined with pressures by the Western Allies upon the Spanish government to prove its neutrality. Commencing with the men who had served the longest at the front, the repatriation of the Division to Spain began. Two trains per week departed from the station at Volosovo. After changing uniforms at Hof, in Bavaria, the first draft of 800 repatriates crossed the Spanish frontier on 29 October 1943. A military band greeted them at Irún, but there were fewer people to welcome them home than had bidden farewell to the departing volunteers two years before.

As repatriation of the Division continued, officers called for volunteers from amongst the single men to remain with the Volunteer Legion, or 'Blue Legion' as it was unofficially known. Surprisingly, it was common to find 50 or more volunteers from one company. The Spanish Ministry of Foreign Affairs and the Ministry of the Army were unable to agree as to the size of the proposed Legion. In desperation, Esteban Infantes despatched Lieutenant-Colonel Díaz de Villegas by plane to Madrid, where, on the morning of 4 November, he was granted a meeting with General Franco, who gave him a decision within 20 minutes. The Legion was to

A small gift for modellers! The name-board of the Blue Division's General Headquarters at Grigorovo. (Bundesarchiv, Koblenz)

number between 1,000 to 1,500. This meant that there were volunteers to spare. Leaving Díaz de Villegas in command of the remnants of the Division, Esteban Infantes flew to Berlin on 16 November to conclude arrangements with the German High Command regarding the Division, the Legion and the many Spanish service organizations.

On 23 December General Esteban Infantes flew home to Madrid, and the following morning Lieutenant-Colonel Díaz de Villegas boarded a Junkers Ju88 at Nikolayevka, the last soldier of the Blue Division to leave the front. Behind there remained only the Blue Legion, and the dead. In just over two years of war the Blue Division had suffered a total of 12,726 casualties, comprising 3,934 dead, 8,466 wounded and 326 missing.

Artillery unit passing through a Russian town; the Spanish arm shield is just visible on the lead rider. All artillery in the Division was horse-drawn. (Author's collection)

The Blue Squadron and the Blue Legion

Another unit which served with distinction was the Spanish Expeditionary Air Squadron (Blue Squadron)—in fact, five squadrons which relieved one another consecutively, commanded by Comandantes Salas, Salvador, Ferrándiz, Cuadra and Galarza. The squadron operated in support of Army Group Centre, being attached to JG27 and later JG51. Its principal mission was the protection of German bombers, the most outstanding actions being fought by the 1st Squadron in the advance on Moscow, and the subsequent retreat, and the 4th in the retreat from Kharkov and the crucial combats over Kursk and Smolensk. The Spanish pilots flew Messerschmitt Bf109 fighters until the end of 1942, when the 3rd Squadron was supplied with Focke-Wulf Fw190s. They shot down a total of 156 Soviet aircraft; Comandante Salas personally scored seven kills and Comandante Cuadra ten. Twenty-two squadron personnel were reported dead or missing, one of whom was eventually repatriated as a prisoner of war.

By 20 November 1943, while the Blue Division was continuing its process of repatriation, the 1,500 volunteers for the Blue Legion had assembled in the barracks at Yamberg on the Latvian frontier. The Legion, commanded by Colonel Antonio García Navarro, consisted of headquarters staff; the 1st and 2nd Infantry Banderas (Spanish designation for a unit smaller than a normal battalion), commanded by Comandantes Ibarra and García respectively; and a 3rd Mixed Bandera with three companies of artillery, anti-tank guns and combined sappers, signallers and reconnaissance, under the command of Comandante Virgili.

After initial operations against partisans around the roads leading to Narva, the Legion was transported eastwards to Begolovo, Schapki and Kostovo, where it was attached to the German 121st Division. Manning an 11-kilometre front, the Spaniards repulsed two strong Soviet assaults on 24 and 25 December, in bitter winter

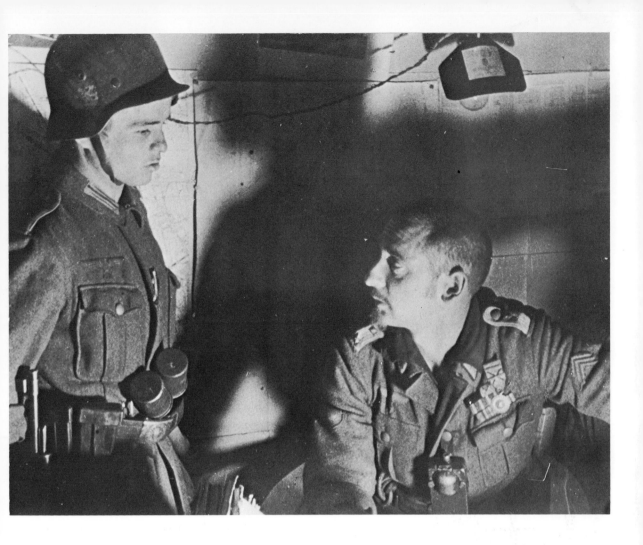

weather. As 1944 began, the entire northern front was collapsing under relentless Russian pressure. The encirclement of Leningrad was abandoned and a general retreat began. On 19 January the Legion was ordered to withdraw southwards and commenced a slow, hard march through freezing wind and snow, fighting off the attacks of partisans. Passing through Ljuban, Sapoldje and Oredesch, the Legion's retreat continued until it reached Luga on the last day of January. From Luga the unit left by train for the Taps-Aiguidu zone in Estonia. Here the Spaniards were re-equipped to defend the Narva coast against possible Soviet landings, only to find that an agreement had been reached between the Spanish and German governments to repatriate the Legion to Spain. On 21 March the Legion departed in trains towards Königsberg, from where it continued by rail until, on 17 April

Something of the fatigue of combat is captured in this photo of a soldier of the Division reporting to his company commander in a command post somewhere south of Leningrad, November 1942. The private has a badly worn Spanish shield decal on his helmet. The lieutenant, a German Army flashlight suspended from his tunic button, displays a mixture of German and Spanish insignia. The habit of wearing the shirt collar open over the tunic was characteristically Spanish. One can make out the national shield on his right sleeve and three wound chevrons on the left one; the Medal of Suffering for the Country, another combat wound decoration, hangs over ribbons which include the Red Cross of Military Merit, the 1936–39 Campaign Medal, and the Individual Military Medal. (Martin Windrow)

1944, the Blue Legion crossed the frontier into Spain.

So ended official Spanish participation in Hitler's war against Russia. However, some former members of the Blue Division and Legion could not forget the struggle still being waged in the east by their erstwhile German comrades-in-

General Emilio Esteban Infantes (right) in conference with the commander of a German flanking division, early in 1943. His Individual Military Medal is worn on the left breast. (Author's collection)

arms. General Franco had ordered that the frontier with France be closed to would-be volunteers, but in small groups some 150 young Spaniards achieved clandestine crossings. Once they were in France, the German authorities facilitated their passage to a training camp at Stablatt, near Königsberg, from where, along with 100 other Spaniards who had remained in Germany, they were incorporated into units of the Waffen SS. In April 1945 a former Blue Division Captain, Miguel Ezquerra, who was now an SS Colonel, commanded three companies of Spaniards plus some survivors from Belgian and French SS Divisions. The men of the 'Unit Ezquerra' were amongst the last troops fighting the Russians in the rubble around Hitler's

Chancellery in Berlin. Though taken prisoner, Ezquerra made a miraculous escape all the way home to Spain.

When the guns finally fell silent in Europe in May 1945, the Western Allies found themselves face to face with a hostile Soviet Union in the middle of a defeated and devastated Germany. The horrors of the Nazi concentration camps were revealed to the world, but for many Europeans the nightmare was far from over. Deportations, executions and starvation continued to bring death in the first years of peace to millions of Germans, Cossacks and others on the losing side, and millions more suffered interminable privations in Soviet labour-camps.

Approximately 350 Spaniards had been taken prisoner or had otherwise gone missing on the Russian front, most of them at the battle of Krasny Bor. The prisoners were incarcerated in 16 Soviet prisons and concentration camps across 7,000 kilometres of territory from Siberia to

Odessa. Despite the long years of brutally hard work, hunger and sometimes harsh punishment, the majority of the prisoners maintained a high morale. Many, however, became so weak that they did not survive. With the death of Stalin in March 1953 there was an improvement in treatment and rumours of possible repatriation. A year later, in March 1954, the Spanish prisoners were assembled in Odessa from their different camps. Ninety-four of the original captives were known to have died, and those now awaiting repatriation numbered 219 men from the Division, seven from the Legion, 21 from the SS and one from the Expeditionary Air Squadron.

On 2 April 1954 the Greek steamer *Semiramis* docked in Barcelona harbour and, after an absence of between 11 and 13 years, the last soldiers of the Blue Division returned to Spanish soil.

The Plates

A1: Captain, Spanish Infantry, June 1941
In 1941 Spanish Army uniforms were still of the pattern worn by the victorious Nationalist Army of the Civil War. This captain wears a khaki-green parade uniform with brown leather buttons and equipment. The three six-pointed gold stars of his rank are worn on the band of his peaked cap and above the Polish cuffs of his tunic, while the infantry branch badge of a bugle-horn with crossed sword and musket is shown on the cap's crown and on both tunic collar points. On his left breast is pinned the Individual Military Medal.

A2: Falangist girl, June 1941
The Feminine Section of the Falange was very active both during and following the Civil War in 'Social Aid'. It also supplied nurses to serve in Russia, the first group of volunteers being organized at the end of July 1941. The girl illustrated wears the red beret and dark blue shirt of the National Movement, a white overall with the red yoke-and-arrows emblem, and a black skirt.

A3: Falangist, June 1941
Also prominent amongst the volunteers were party members of the Falange Española and Civil War ex-combatants. This man wears a dark blue Falangist shirt, displaying both the badge of the SEU and the red yoke-and-arrows in addition to the Campaign Medal (1936–39). On the left upper sleeve is the white inverted chevron of a Falangist front-line combatant. The yoke-and-arrows emblem again appears embossed on the

Rifleman of the Ski Company returning from a reconnaissance on the Leningrad front during winter 1942–43. For their second winter in Russia the Division received supplies of the German padded, reversible camouflage suit. (Author's collection)

silver-grey buckle-plate of the black leather belt. Behind him is a banner carried during a mass demonstration in Madrid on 24 June 1941: 'Falangist Volunteers Against Russia'.

A4: University Militiaman, June 1941

Formed under the auspices of the Falangist SEU (Sindicato Español Universitario), the University Militia received its first uniform in 1941. Light grey in colour, the tunic has red patches on the upper lapels, and gold buttons. Leather equipment is black, and white gloves are worn on parade. Note the 'gaiter'-straps at the foot of the

Mercedes Milá Nolla, appointed by Franco in 1937 as Inspector General of Women Auxiliaries of the 'Sanidad Militar', in conference with Lt.-Col. Pellicer, Inspector of Hospitals, during a visit to the front in summer 1943. The caduceus symbol can just be seen on his shoulder-strap. She wears a Spanish Red Cross badge on the left breast, above the Red Military Merit Cross and the 1936–39 Campaign Medal. (Author's collection)

trousers. The forage cap displays the emblem of the SEU—a white eagle with a blue-and-white chequered shield superimposed and the red yoke-and-arrows symbol of the Falange behind its head. A dark blue shirt and black tie complete the uniform, and the weapon is a Mauser Gewehr 98 rifle. A high percentage of volunteers for the Blue Division came from the universities.

B1: Lieutenant, Artillery, July 1941

The dress of the Spanish volunteers, from their formation in Spain until they reached their training camp in Germany, was a mixture of Spanish Army uniform and the apparel of the National Movement. This lieutenant wears a red beret, khaki-green tunic, light khaki breeches reinforced with leather on the inside leg, and brown leather equipment. Two six-pointed gold stars of rank are shown on beret and sleeves, and the artillery branch badge of a bursting shell is worn on both collar points. On his left breast are the Campaign

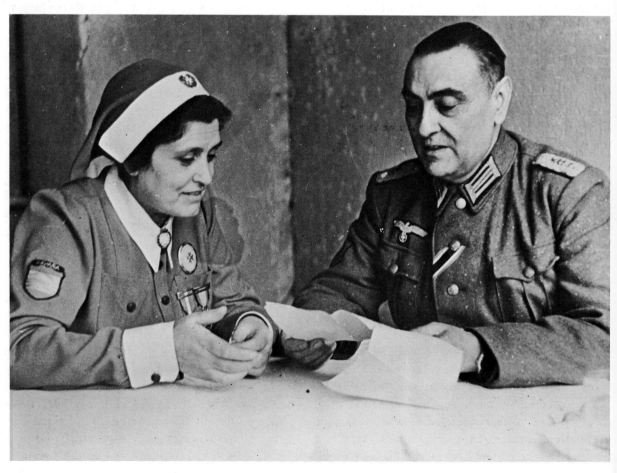

Medal (1936–39) and the Red Military Merit Cross. Many Army officers preferred to continue wearing their khaki shirts rather than the Falangist blue shirt.

B2: Corporal, Infantry, July 1941
This man wears khaki-green uniform and canvas anklets. His buttons and leather equipment are brown. The red beret and tunic collar points display the infantry branch badge, as does the gold buckle-plate of his belt. On each lower sleeve he wears the three slanting red stripes of his rank, and above his left breast pocket is pinned the Campaign Medal (1936–39). The dark blue collar of his Falangist shirt is worn outside the tunic collar. He carries the flag of the 2nd Battalion, Regiment Pimentel, Spanish Volunteer Division.

B3: Sapper, July 1941
Dressed identically to the previous figure in all principal items, this soldier wears the sappers' branch badge of a silver castle on his beret and tunic collar points. His left breast pocket shows a blue patch bearing the red yoke-and-arrows emblem, while above the pocket can be seen the 'detente' or badge of the Sacred Heart of Jesus. A rolled blanket is slung over his shoulder in the traditional Spanish manner.

C1: Infantryman, winter 1941–42
At the front, regulation German uniforms and equipment were worn. During the first winter the most common dress was the field-grey woollen toque (balaclava) and greatcoat, shown here with the Spanish national shield worn on the right upper sleeve. The shield is in the Spanish colours of red and gold with 'España' inscribed in gold at the top. This figure wears the dark grey trousers which were normal issue prior to 1942. Although German infantrymen were at that time equipped with three-quarter-length leather boots, the Spanish volunteers were dismayed to find that the classical 'marching boots' were to be denied them and that they would have to make do with black lace-up ankle-boots and green canvas anklets. The soldier depicted is also wearing a regulation German Army belt supporting a black leather machine gun case (for tools and acces-

sories) and a holstered pistol. Over his shoulder is slung the commonly-used 7.92mm MG.34 light machine gun and a 50-round continuous-link ammunition belt.

C2: Sergeant, Ski Company, winter 1942–43
The Ski Company was first formed towards the end of 1941 to patrol the west shore of Lake Ilmen, which was subject to frequent infiltrations by Soviet ski troops. Early attempts at snow camouflage were achieved with white sheets, shirts and even long underwear. A year later, however, the Spanish volunteers—like the rest of the German Army—were better supplied. The sergeant illustrated wears over his uniform a white two-piece snow suit with white buttons and an attached hood. The trousers are tied with tape around the top of his black, thick-soled ski-boots. Covering his head and neck is a separate, reversible, thick-lined hood, tied with two tapes at the front. Snow-goggles and leather gauntlets provide additional protection. On his left breast the sergeant has stitched the Spanish insignia of his rank—three gold horizontal stripes. Officially (and normally) only German rank insignia was worn, but the Spaniards—resentful that they were not allowed to fight in Spanish uniforms—were inclined to adorn themselves with items of their own national insignia, apparently at whim and to a degree never attempted by other foreign volunteers. Attached to his belt are his black leather holster, containing a 9mm '08 Parabellum pistol (pistols were issued only to officers, sergeants and light machine gun teams) and green canvas magazine pouches for the 9mm MP.40 sub-machine gun which he carries slung across his chest.

C3: Soldier of Reconnaissance Group, winter 1942–43
The 250th Reconnaissance Group was organized in squadrons like a cavalry formation. All of its officers were volunteers from the Spanish Cavalry Corps, as were some of the other ranks. The soldier depicted wears (unofficially) his Spanish Army brown leather belt with the cavalry branch badge of crossed swords and lances beneath a crown on the silver buckle-plate. He is dressed in a reversible two-piece snow suit, which was considerably thicker and warmer than that worn by

the previous figure. The jacket is double-breasted and has an adjustable, reversible hood. The cuffs of the sleeves and the bottom of both the jacket and the trouser legs all have draw-strings to tighten and secure as required. He also wears a white cloth cover over his steel helmet, and regulation German Y-straps. Equipment shown includes gas mask container, aluminium mess tin and water-bottle. He is armed with a captured Soviet 7.62mm PPSh.41 sub-machine gun, which was an extremely popular weapon in the Blue Division. It could be loaded with either a 71-round drum or a 35-round box magazine and could fire 105 rounds per minute on full automatic.

Men of the 262nd Regt. pay their respects to comrades who are staying in Russia; an *Alférez*, or Ensign, lies between two privates. (Bundesarchiv, Koblenz)

D1 : Sergeant of Sappers, summer 1942

During formation the competition to obtain places in the Blue Division was so keen that many serving officers and NCOs agreed to serve in ranks greatly inferior to those they currently held. The volunteer depicted here, however, appears to have regained the rank he had previously held in the Falangist militia. On his folded field-grey tunic the dark blue-green epaulette, with a border of silver-grey braiding (*Tresse*), shows his rank as that of sergeant (*Unterfeldwebel*). This is matched by the three gold stripes above the pocket of his shirt—the Spanish Army insignia for sergeant—while beneath the pocket the two red arrows on a black background represent the Falangist militia equivalent to sergeant—*Subjefe de Falange*. The piping on the epaulette, the two 'lights' on each of the grey collar patches, and the inverted chevron over the German national

34

cockade on the 1938 pattern field cap are all black—the sappers' branch colour. The grey German eagle emblem can also be seen on both cap and tunic. The dark blue shirt displays the red yoke-and-arrows on the left pocket and the white inverted chevron of a Falangist front-line combatant on the upper sleeve. Note the green mosquito net covering his head and shoulders.

D2: Artilleryman, summer 1942
This soldier wears field-grey uniform and steel helmet and black riding boots with spurs. His tunic shows the Spanish national shield and the grey German eagle emblem. The epaulettes are piped with bright red artillery branch colour (*Waffenfarbe*) and the grey collar patches each have two 'lights' of the same colour. Slung over his shoulder is a Mauser Kar.98k rifle. He is mounted on the lead horse of the team.

D3: Lieutenant, Expeditionary Air Squadron, 1942
Many Civil War aces jumped at the chance to see more action in the skies over Russia. This fighter-pilot wears standard Luftwaffe grey-blue flying uniform. His field cap displays silver-grey officer's piping and the Luftwaffe eagle, and the cockade of German national colours—red, white and black. His collar rank patches each show two silver-grey eagles and laurels on a golden-yellow background with silver-grey cord piping round the edge, while his silver braid epaulettes on yellow backing each have a four-pointed gold rank star in the centre. The right sleeve of the flight blouse displays the Spanish national shield. Below the silver-grey Luftwaffe eagle on the right breast is the emblem of the SEU, while above can be seen the silver metal pilot's badge of the Spanish Air Force. On the left breast are pinned the Individual Military Medal and the German pilot-observer's badge. He wears black leather and suede flying boots and holds a brown leather flying helmet with fleece-lined interior.

E1: General Muñoz Grandes, February 1942
True to his reputation for unconventional dress during the Civil War, General Muñoz Grandes is here wearing an other ranks' field cap minus the gold piping on the turn-up edge to which a general was normally entitled. The gold eagle on

Returned veterans, garlanded with flowers, drive through Madrid on 25 May 1942. The right-hand man can be seen to wear the Spanish arm shield, and the second from the left has the German eagle badge on his red beret. (Author's collection)

his cap is worn above an inverted gold chevron and the German national cockade. His field-grey other ranks' tunic has gold buttons and a gold German eagle emblem, general's collar patches of gold oak leaves on a bright red background, and epaulettes of gold and silver cord on a background of bright red. Also displayed are the Iron Cross 1st Class; the ribbon of the Iron Cross 2nd Class; and the Spanish national arm shield, worn here with a metal yoke-and-arrows badge pinned over it.

E2: Captain, Infantry, 1942
This wounded officer wears a field-grey peaked *Schirmmütze* with a dark blue-green band, white infantry piping, silver cords and buttons, a white metal German national eagle, and a white metal oak leaf cluster with the cockade in the centre. The dark blue-green collar of the field-grey tunic has silver-grey collar *Litzen* with two white 'lights' on each, and the eagle emblem over the right pocket is also silver-grey. The epaulettes are of silver-grey braid on white backing with two gold rank stars on each. The right sleeve shows the Spanish national shield, and the left pocket a small metal yoke-and-arrows badge. Above this pocket are the ribbons for the Campaign Medal (1936–39) and the Red Military Merit Cross, while fixed to the second top button-hole is the ribbon of the Iron Cross 2nd Class. His field-grey

breeches have dark grey leather reinforcing the inside leg.

E3: Nurse of 'Sanidad Militar', 1942

The Division's seriously sick and wounded were treated at hospitals in Mestelevo, Riga, Vilna, Königsberg, Berlin and Hof, operated principally by Spanish medical staff, who included many volunteer nurses from the Spanish Army and the Falange's Feminine Section. The Army nurse depicted here is wearing a headdress of khaki wimple and white coif, upon which is pinned a silver-grey metal badge of the Spanish Army's medical branch—'Sanidad Militar'. Her khaki blouse has a white collar and cuffs and dark brown leather buttons. Displayed at the throat is the emblem of the Spanish Red Cross, and on the left breast Franco's Civil War award to Women Auxiliaries of 'Sanidad Militar', the Campaign Medal (1936–39) and the Red Military Merit Cross. She also wears a black belt with a silver-grey 'Sanidad Militar' buckle-plate, a pleated khaki skirt, light brown stockings and dark brown shoes.

F1: Standard-bearer, Infantry, 1942

This figure wears a field-grey Model 1935 steel helmet with a shield decal in the Spanish national colours. His uniform is also field-grey. The grey collar patches each have two 'lights' of infantry white, and the collar, interestingly, is bordered by a double width of narrow silver-grey braid. Displayed on the tunic are the German eagle emblem, the ribbons of the Campaign Medal (1936–39), the Individual Military Medal and the Red Military Merit Cross; the Medal of Suffering for the Country (wounded by enemy fire), and the Medal of Knights Maimed in War for the Country. The standard-bearer's bandolier and 'bucket' is in the Spanish national colours and passes from his left shoulder to his right side, beside the brown leather map-case. In the centre of his chest is strapped a field-grey gas-cape bag, while suspended from the left side of his belt are triple green canvas sub-machine gun magazine pouches complete with filling tool pocket, a

Another group of veterans in the same parade, wearing sappers' branch badges on their collars. The lieutenant on the left has his rank stars on a black 'biscuit' over his left pocket, and above this a sapper's emblem of no particular significance. The right sleeve patch, interestingly, appears to be that of the Aragón Army Corps during the Civil War. (Author's collection)

bayonet frog and a white bayonet knot, the colour indicating that the soldier is in the 1st Battalion of his regiment. The standard he is holding is in the Spanish national colours, and is the flag of the 1st Battalion of the 269th Regiment.

F2: Private, Infantry Battalion of the Ministry of the Army, December 1941

Each Christmas a train-load of brandy, wine and seasonal fare—General Franco's gift to the Spanish Volunteer Division—arrived at the front, escorted by men of the élite Infantry Battalion of the Ministry of the Army in Madrid. This soldier wears the khaki-green walking-out uniform of the Spanish Army. The peaked cap has a brown leather strap and gold buttons. The double-breasted, pleated greatcoat also has gold buttons and the sleeves have Polish cuffs. The badge seen on the crown of the cap, as well as on the epaulettes and collar points of the greatcoat, is the emblem of the Spanish ground forces—the crowned, gold eagle of St John the Evangelist with the red cross of St James in the centre. His right sleeve shows the Spanish national shield.

Red, gold and black Spanish national arm shield worn by all ranks of the Blue Division on the upper right sleeve. (Author's collection)

F3: Soldier of Assault Platoon, winter 1942–43

Each regiment had an Assault Platoon which undertook special attack and demolition missions. The soldier illustrated is dressed in a single-piece snow overall, worn over his uniform, with an attached hood and white buttons down the front. He wears a regulation German Army belt with a Stielgranate 24 stick grenade under it, while on his head is a grey Russian fleece cap, taken from the enemy, upon which he has pinned a metal yoke-and-arrows badge. Also captured from the enemy is the Soviet 7.62mm Degtyarev DP light machine gun and canvas magazine satchel. The DP had a 47-round drum magazine and, although not having the high rate of fire of the German MG.34, was none the less highly favoured by the Assault Platoons due to its simplicity and reliability.

G1: Brigada, Infantry, May 1942

The first expedition of 1,300 of the longest-serving combatants arrived back in Spain in May 1942 wearing a uniform which differed in some

respects from the one in which they had departed nearly a year before. This Brigada (sergeant-major) is wearing a khaki-green Spanish uniform with a grey German eagle emblem over the right breast pocket as well as on the front of his red beret. Also on his beret and at the base of his cuff are the two vertical gold stripes of his rank. Spanish infantry branch badges are worn on the collar points of the tunic, which has brown buttons, and bears the Spanish national shield, the red yoke-and-arrows emblem and the Individual Military Medal. The dark blue collar of his Falangist shirt is visible outside the tunic collar, and his brown belt has a gold buckle-plate embossed with the infantry branch badge. His trousers are tucked into his brown ankle-boots.

G2: Captain, Spanish Air Force, summer 1942

Upon returning to service with the Spanish armed forces, the Russian Front veterans were

Some of the 1,300 returned veterans attending a Thanks-giving Mass in Retiro Park, Madrid; the three infantry officers in the foreground all wear the Iron Cross. The captain, right, has three wound chevrons on his left upper sleeve, and just visible on his left forearm in the original print are two separate awards of the Collective Military Medal. (Author's collection)

authorized to wear their arm shields and German decorations on their Spanish uniforms. The Air Force captain illustrated wears the light blue summer uniform with gold buttons, a white shirt and a dark blue tie. The three six-pointed gold stars of his rank are shown on the band of his peaked cap above a gold strap and button, and also on each lower sleeve of the tunic above the gold pointed piping on the cuffs. The silver metal pilot's badge is worn on the crown of the cap and over the right breast pocket, and the Spanish national shield on the right sleeve. In line on his left upper breast are the Campaign Medal (1936–39), the Red Military Merit Cross and the Medal of Suffering for the Country (wounded by enemy fire). Above is the German Front Flight Bar and, below, the Spanish War Cross and the German pilot-observer's badge. Suspended from the second top buttonhole is the Iron Cross 2nd Class.

G3: Lieutenant, Infantry, May 1942
Many of the returned veterans did not wear the German eagle emblem, as evidenced by this officer, depicted in attendance at the Thanks-giving Mass held for the expedition in the Retiro Park, Madrid. His rank is shown by the two six-pointed gold stars on the red patch (the Spanish infantry branch colour) above the left breast pocket of his khaki-green tunic, and by the two stars on his red beret. Also displayed on the tunic are the German War Cross with Swords, the Infantry Assault Badge and the Iron Cross 2nd Class; in Spanish style the cross itself is worn. The right upper sleeve would bear the Spanish national shield, while on the left upper sleeve are three gold wound stripes and on the lower sleeve the green and red cloth badge of the Collective Military Medal. His shirt collar is dark blue and his leather equipment brown.

H1: Chaplain, 1943

Twenty-four members of the Spanish Army's Ecclesiastic Corps volunteered for the Blue Division in July 1941. As all religious festivals and practices were observed by the Spanish volunteers, even in the front line, the chaplains' services were in great demand. Wearing a uniform almost identical to his German counterparts, this Spanish chaplain has a field-grey peaked service cap with violet piping (the ecclesiastic branch colour) round the crown and lining both edges of the dark blue-green cap band. The cap cords and buttons are silver, as are the metal German eagle emblem and small Gothic cross on the crown. Beneath these, on the cap band, are the silver metal oak leaf cluster and the German national cockade. The field-grey tunic is without epaulettes and has silver buttons. The silver collar *Litzen* on violet backing cloth have two purple 'lights' on each, and there is a silver German eagle emblem over the right pocket. While German chaplains wore no rank insignia, the Spanish were given permission, after some argument, to show their grades on a violet patch over the left breast pocket, in the Spanish style; this figure wears the three gold stars of a captain. Also on display are the badge of the Sacred Heart, the ribbon of the Iron Cross 2nd Class, and the Spanish national shield. Round his neck is a violet stole with a gold border and a gold cross at each end. The crucifix is of the type used by the Spanish Army, and is on a gold chain.

H2: Grenadier of Waffen-SS 'Unit Ezquerra', April 1945

This veteran is dressed in the 1944 pattern field blouse and 1943 field cap. On the front of the cap is a field-grey cloth patch with silver-grey SS eagle and death's-head insignia. His right collar shows the silver-grey SS runes on a black patch, while the plain black patch on the left indicates private's rank. White infantry *Waffenfarbe* piping borders the black epaulettes. On the left upper sleeve are worn the silver-grey SS eagle emblem and the Spanish national shield. On display across his chest are the ribbon of the Iron Cross 2nd Class, the Spanish government's medal for Spanish Volunteers in Russia, and the Iron Cross 1st Class. Above is the Close Combat Bar

Three medals to which men of the Blue Division were entitled. *(Left)* German commemorative medal for the Blue Division, not issued until 1944; the reverse is enscribed 'Division Española de Voluntarios en Rusia'. Narrow black and white sidestripes flank broad red stripes with a gold centre. *(Middle)* The Spanish Volunteers in Russia Medal, issued by the Spanish government in 1942. The reverse of the crowned eagle of St John the Evangelist shows Kremlin towers, and 'Rusia 1941'. The ribbon is white, flanked with red/gold/red on the left, and black/white/red/white/black on the right. *(Right)* The familiar German medal issued in 1942 to all personnel who fought in the first winter of the Russian campaign; its ribbon is red with white and black central stripes, and the reverse is inscribed 'Winterschlacht im Osten 1941/42'. (Author's collection)

in bronze and, below, the Infantry Assault Badge. The regulation SS belt supports the black leather ammunition pouches for the 7.92mm Mauser Kar.98k rifle.

H3: Company flag of the 3rd Battalion, 263rd Regiment

A variety of battalion and company flags was manufactured in Spain for the Blue Division. Early flags bore the regiment's number or the name of its commander and the title 'Spanish Volunteer Division'. Later, when the Division was at the front, battalion flags were in the Spanish national colours of red and gold, with the numbered regiment and battalion in black lettering above and below the Spanish coat of arms. The company flag illustrated displays a German Iron Cross and the Falangist yoke-and-arrows superimposed on the Spanish national shield. Above is the by-then accepted title 'Blue Division', and below '263rd Regiment—3rd Battalion', all on a background of the red-and-black colours of the Falange.

INDEX

(References to illustrations are shown in **bold**. Plates are prefixed 'pl.' with commentary locators in brackets.)

COMPANION SERIES FROM OSPREY

ESSENTIAL HISTORIES
Concise studies of the motives, methods and repercussions of human conflict, spanning history from ancient times to the present day. Each volume studies one major war or arena of war, providing an indispensable guide to the fighting itself, the people involved, and its lasting impact on the world around it.

CAMPAIGN
Accounts of history's greatest conflicts, detailing the command strategies, tactics, movements and actions of the opposing forces throughout the crucial stages of each campaign. Full-colour battle scenes, 3-dimensional 'bird's-eye views', photographs and battle maps guide the reader through each engagement from its origins to its conclusion.

ORDER OF BATTLE
The greatest battles in history, featuring unit-by-unit examinations of the troops and their movements as well as analysis of the commanders' original objectives and actual achievements. Colour maps including a large fold-out base map, organisational diagrams and photographs help the reader to trace the course of the fighting in unprecedented detail.

ELITE
This series focuses on uniforms, equipment, insignia and unit histories in the same way as Men-at-Arms but in more extended treatments of larger subjects, also including personalities and techniques of warfare.

NEW VANGUARD
The design, development, operation and history of the machinery of warfare through the ages. Photographs, full-colour artwork and cutaway drawings support detailed examinations of the most significant mechanical innovations in the history of human conflict.

WARRIOR
Insights into the daily lives of history's fighting men and women, past and present, detailing their motivation, training, tactics, weaponry and experiences. Meticulously researched narrative and full-colour artwork, photographs, and scenes of battle and daily life provide detailed accounts of the experiences of combatants through the ages.

AIRCRAFT OF THE ACES
Portraits of the elite pilots of the 20th century's major air campaigns, including unique interviews with surviving aces. Unit listings, scale plans and full-colour artwork combine with the best archival photography available to provide a detailed insight into the experience of war in the air.

COMBAT AIRCRAFT
The world's greatest military aircraft and combat units and their crews, examined in detail. Each exploration of the leading technology, men and machines of aviation history is supported by unit listings and other data, artwork, scale plans, and archival photography.